I AM | *Positively Grateful*
Gratitude Journal

Published in 2018 by Warrior Woman Media

Copyright © I Am | Jen Wilson & Warrior Woman Project® 2018

Jen Wilson has asserted her right to be identified as the author of this Work in accordance with the Copyright, Designs and Patents Act 1988

ISBN Paperback: 978-0-9957070-3-0

All rights reserved. No part of this publication may be reproduces, stored in a retrieval system, or transmitted in any form or by any means, electronic, mechanical, photocopying, recording or otherwise, without the prior permission of the copyright owner.

Positively Grateful Journal

So what is this journal about?

This journal is to help you make some time for YOU each day. Getting positive and clear on the things you are grateful for. Life will throw us curve balls all the time, learning to focus on gratitude and positive outcomes is teaching us to be resilient and helps us to know which bat to pick up to hit the ball out the park (or which foot to kick with). There is a whole lot of neuro science confirming the positive benefits of gratitude and the information is updating all the time. You just need to do a search online to find loads of links to the research.

Sections in the journal

The pages haven't been dated so you can start your journal whenever the hell you like. Who says your New Year HAS to start on 01 Jan? Break the rules (if that is what you like to do) or start on 01st Jan, it's your life and your journal.

Values. Know your values, when you know who you are and what you are about life gets a whole lot easier to understand. When you know and live by your values decisions are easier to make, and your relationships with everyone are easier to understand. If you have read my book Become a Warrior Woman, 9 Rules to Sort Your Shit you will already have worked through this task and have your lists, if you haven't you can grab a copy over on Amazon. I think it is really important to get clear on the definition of each of your values so YOU know what they mean and you clearly recognise them.

The Questions

How do I feel today and what do I need to do to show me some love?

This allows you to stop for a moment to check in with yourself, your mood, your energy and think about the action you need to take to come from a place of love. Depending on where you and the moon are in your cycle could affect your mood and energy. Also how your sleep has been, how your diet is and your stress levels. It's good to keep track.

If you wake up feeling low energy because you've had a bad night sleep or bad dreams, or you just feel down and you are not sure why, take the time to acknowledge this and let go of anything that will bring you down through the rest of the day. Writing out your thoughts really can help clear them or give you clarity on what's going on.

It can also be useful to track your monthly cycle and the moon cycles. Both of these are extremely powerful. You may start to notice a pattern of your energy and mindset being up and down. Once you understand that, you can start to make it work in your favour. All humans live in a cycle, women tend to be more in tune and notice more fluctuations but it's not unique to us women alone. Knowing and understanding these cycles and yourself is POWERFUL stuff!

Your energy and mood can also be impacted by future events. You might have a meeting or event happen later in the day that you are not looking forward to. Take the time to remember the things that you're looking forward to and remember that you have the choice always of how you react to a situation. Allow yourself to feel emotions and understand why you feel the way you do. You're a human being and emotions are part of that cycle, learning about vulnerability and allowing myself to be and to feel has been a huge part of my growth cycle in the last few years. I only really learned and understood what vulnerability was around 2014/15!

Bring some focus in to the positives that you have coming up in the day. Maybe you get to make a really nice lunch, or arrange to meet a friend who makes you laugh, or wear an outfit that makes you feel good (you should ideally always feel good in your clothes regardless if its joggies and a hoodie or a glam dress, I have friends who are style coaches who will tell you to bin anything you don't feel great in, I 100% agree with them). Maybe you day allows you get to go for a run, punch something, stay in your jammies all day watching movies... Only you know what you can do to show yourself some love and put a smile on your beautiful face.

Morning Gratitude & Intentions. Spend a few minutes in the morning to remind yourself of what you are grateful for and set a positive intention so your focus is helping you approach the day from a place of love.

Think of something you are grateful for and WHY – this is important to really amplify the benefits of gratitude. It can be anything from your cosy bed, the mornings getting lighter (depending on the time of year), getting to go to work (because you actually have a job), having a day off because we all need regular rest, having love in your life, breath in your lungs, meeting a friend later for coffee or dinner... whatever you are grateful for.

If this is the first time you have done any gratitude journaling don't get stressed, there are no rules and once you start practicing gratitude you will notice more things. If you are getting stuck... what allows you to have what you are grateful for? The job you have, the skills you have learned to do that job, your physical health that gets you to work, your senses to be able to touch, feel, see, hear, smell your life experiences, the people that grew the cotton and farmed the cotton and made your sheets and got it transported to the shops and the person that served you and packed it... there really is more to a warm cosy bed than just the warm cosy bed...

The most successful people in the world and all of the happiest people in the world practice gratitude every single day - join our gang, it's a good place to be.

The more you practice, the easier it becomes. Research using MRI scans actually show areas of the brain get thicker when you practice these positive actions (and not just gratitude, meditation also thickens areas of the brain when regularly practiced). In simple terms when that area of your brain thickens, it strengthens the path and over time it will become second nature to be that way whether it is grateful, compassionate, loving, or positive. Our brains are intuitively tuned to protect us and that usually means negativity and fear are go to places. The good news is thought that with conscious effort to turn it to positive is possible (science has proven it).

It's not woo woo, hippy dippy, it is real science!

Next set 3 positive intentions to make your day awesome. There are no rules other than write in a positive and present tense to help your brain know these are happening.

For example: I am drinking at least 2 litres of water today. I am meditating and letting go of shit that usually winds me up. I am eating a healthy lunch and really enjoying it. I am rocking it out at my fitness class. I am dealing with my boss with an easy breezy attitude. I am dancing to my favourite music to raise my energy and universal vibration... You get the idea.

Evening Evaluations. Spend a few minutes in the evening reflecting. Be proud of at least one thing and write why and take one lesson from the day. This gives you space to review, appreciate, celebrate, reflect and learn.

When we take a lesson from the day, even what seems like the shittiest of days turns out to be good. So often when we think we have had a bad day, it's really only been a very small portion of that day that has left us feeling on a low vibe. When we acknowledge that we are getting to tune back in to gratitude and positive energy to help lift us up.

Acknowledge how you feel daily. Be honest with yourself about how you feel. Some days you wake up feeling shitty. Then you are going to think about what you need to do to turn that around in to a positive.

Free Flow Thoughts

A blank page for you to free flow whatever you want to write, draw, doodle... It can be really beneficial to work out what is going on in your head when you write. I find it really useful to not think too much about what I am writing and just let the words flow out. It can give some real clarity to what's going on. Write, draw, colour, scribble... When I do my tarot cards I like to keep track of them here too.

My Story & This Journal

If you have read my first book Become A Warrior Woman 9 Rules to Sort Your Shit you will know my creation story, if you haven't read it, you should, it's a really good book! It will give you my 9 Rules and more tools to make this journal even more effective.

But to give you the jist of my story: My world fell apart when my marriage ended, I pieced my life back together creating the Warrior Woman Project to help empower women who felt lost and stuck in their lives. For many women self-care and self-love have taken a back seat for family, work, friends, our over demanding world and have either not had the time or have not been prepared to make the time to make themselves happy and feel worthy of care and love. We also use this 'busyness' to avoid dealing with our lives and think everything will work out okay if we can bury our heads in the sand for long enough. I have tried this and believe me, it doesn't work.

If you just want to read that 1st chapter you can download it for FREE over at www.warriorwomanproject.com/freechapter it is available as a PDF and an audio, there is also a FREE 9 Rules online training available that you can access over at www.warriorwomanproject.com/9-Rules-online-training

This journal came together from me losing sight of why those rules are important, why they work and what happened after the Become a Warrior Woman book was released.

On March 11th 2017 at 1005am (a day and time I will never forget) I was diagnosed with Crohn's disease. I had been unwell since October 2016 but nothing really wrong, just a few things that were not right. Then by mid-January things got a whole lot worse and I was really unwell.

Even though my GP had suggested he thought it was inflammatory bowel disease, it wasn't something I expected, and the journey it sent me on wasn't one I thought I had time for – I was too busy. The Universe had other plans and gave me the time, and lots of it. I was in agony and I now know what chronic pain feels like. I had lost over 15KG (2.5 Stones) in weight, I was frail and weak and I couldn't do things like change the sheets on my bed or vacuum the house. Walking was more of a shuffle than a stride and going from the sofa to the toilet was an effort.

I felt helpless and couldn't understand why I was so unwell I was physically strong and healthy, or so I thought. Deep down I knew this was just a passing phase but it was SO hard at the time to get a focus on that. 'This too shall pass' was great advice given to me.

One of the most positive outcomes of being diagnosed with Crohn's disease was it opened me back up to a whole new world of time, research and learning and I was reading academic journals again to deepen my understanding of what was going on in my body, why it was happening and what options were available to me outside of what the consultants and nurses were telling me. I had to focus on what I was grateful on, when I wasn't I was very quickly slipping in to a dark and gloomy place.

I want you to wake up every day, recognise the good stuff going on, love your life and focusing on the things you have to look forward to.

I can't tell you bad things won't happen. They will for sure. And a lot of it is out of our control.

What is in our control is how we choose to respond and react to the situation.

It's about understanding that shit things happen and not allowing that to control our lives. It's up to us to find the best possible outcome of the situation.

The challenges teach us our strengths and resilience, and there will be times that we're sad, angry, hurt, and fucking raging about the shit being thrown at you.

You will want to scream 'why me?? I am a good person!!' – I know I have been there screaming that very phrase. And briefly have that moment BUT, don't wallow in it.

Don't be a victim. Be a Warrior.

During the toughest of days working through this style of journaling helped bring me back to a place where I appreciated what I had and this is why I put it together to help you.

I also went back to the Become a Warrior Woman 9 Rules and had to work through those 9 rules again myself. As much as I had been in a place of self-love and self-care there were still areas of my life that needed work. I don't think there is ever a time when there is not an area that needs work – and that is okay.

I learned from a dear friend who passed away during the time of creating this journal that, once you have done everything you can and your time is up, you need to let go. While you are alive, take every opportunity you can, be curious and explore those curiosities no matter what other people think about it. It's your life to live the way you want. He was one of those guys that made time for people and looked after himself the best he could, and even in his 80's he was always reading, learning, loving and curious about the world and life right to the end.

We have the choice to dwell and be a victim of circumstance or search for meaning and be a Warrior. What do you choose to be?

I hope this journal brings you joy, answers, clarity, direction and hope.

Big love

Jen x

My Life Values

My No. 1 Value is _____

To me it means _____

_____

My No. 2 Value is _____

To me it means _____

_____

My No. 3 Value is _____

To me it means _____

_____

My No. 4 Value is _____

To me it means _____

_____

My No. 5 Value is _____

To me it means _____

_____

My Relationship Values

My No. 1 Value is _____

To me it means _____

_____

My No. 2 Value is _____

To me it means _____

_____

My No. 3 Value is _____

To me it means _____

_____

My No. 4 Value is _____

To me it means _____

_____

My No. 5 Value is _____

To me it means _____

_____

My Career Values

My No. 1 Value is _____

To me it means _____

_____

My No. 2 Value is _____

To me it means _____

_____

My No. 3 Value is _____

To me it means _____

_____

My No. 4 Value is _____

To me it means _____

_____

My No. 5 Value is _____

To me it means _____

_____

My Money Values

My No. 1 Value is _____

To me it means _____

_____

My No. 2 Value is _____

To me it means _____

_____

My No. 3 Value is _____

To me it means _____

_____

My No. 4 Value is _____

To me it means _____

_____

My No. 5 Value is _____

To me It means _____

_____

Day   Date:

Good morning, today I start the day with gratitude and positive intentions.

How do I feel and how will I show myself some love?

_____

_____

1 thing I am grateful for this morning

_____

_____

I am grateful for this because

_____

_____

3 positive intentions for the day to **show myself love…**

1.

2.

3.

Reflect on the day, remember the positive and acknowledge the lessons.

1 thing I am proud of today and why

_____

_____

_____

_____

1 thing I learned today that I will help me grow

_____

_____

Free Flow Thoughts

Day   Date:

Good morning, today I start the day with gratitude and positive intentions.

How do I feel and how will I show myself some love?

_____

_____

1 thing I am grateful for this morning

_____

_____

I am grateful for this because

_____

_____

3 positive intentions for the day to **show myself love...**

1.

2.

3.

Reflect on the day, remember the positive and acknowledge the lessons.

1 thing I am proud of today and why

_____

_____

_____

_____

1 thing I learned today that I will help me grow

_____

_____

Free Flow Thoughts

Day   Date:

Good morning, today I start the day with gratitude and positive intentions.

How do I feel and how will I show myself some love?

_____

_____

1 thing I am grateful for this morning

_____

_____

I am grateful for this because

_____

_____

3 positive intentions for the day to **show myself love...**

1.

2.

3.

Reflect on the day, remember the positive and acknowledge the lessons.

1 thing I am proud of today and why

_____

_____

_____

_____

1 thing I learned today that I will help me grow

_____

_____

Free Flow Thoughts

Day   Date:

Good morning, today I start the day with gratitude and positive intentions.

How do I feel and how will I show myself some love?

_____

_____

1 thing I am grateful for this morning

_____

_____

I am grateful for this because

_____

_____

3 positive intentions for the day to **show myself love**...

1.

2.

3.

Reflect on the day, remember the positive and acknowledge the lessons.

1 thing I am proud of today and why

_____

_____

_____

_____

1 thing I learned today that I will help me grow

_____

_____

Free Flow Thoughts

Day

Date:

Good morning, today I start the day with gratitude and positive intentions.

How do I feel and how will I show myself some love?

_____

_____

1 thing I am grateful for this morning

_____

_____

I am grateful for this because

_____

_____

3 positive intentions for the day to **show myself love...**

1.

2.

3.

Reflect on the day, remember the positive and acknowledge the lessons.

1 thing I am proud of today and why

_____

_____

_____

_____

1 thing I learned today that I will help me grow

_____

_____

Free Flow Thoughts

Day   Date:

Good morning, today I start the day with gratitude and positive intentions.

How do I feel and how will I show myself some love?

_____

_____

1 thing I am grateful for this morning

_____

_____

I am grateful for this because

_____

_____

3 positive intentions for the day to **show myself love…**

1.

2.

3.

Reflect on the day, remember the positive and acknowledge the lessons.

1 thing I am proud of today and why

_____

_____

_____

_____

1 thing I learned today that I will help me grow

_____

_____

Free Flow Thoughts

Day   Date:

Good morning, today I start the day with gratitude and positive intentions.

How do I feel and how will I show myself some love?

_____

_____

1 thing I am grateful for this morning

_____

_____

I am grateful for this because

_____

_____

3 positive intentions for the day to **show myself love...**

1.

2.

3.

Reflect on the day, remember the positive and acknowledge the lessons.

1 thing I am proud of today and why

_____

_____

_____

_____

1 thing I learned today that I will help me grow

_____

_____

Free Flow Thoughts

Day   Date:

Good morning, today I start the day with gratitude and positive intentions.

How do I feel and how will I show myself some love?

_____

_____

1 thing I am grateful for this morning

_____

_____

I am grateful for this because

_____

_____

3 positive intentions for the day to **show myself love…**

1.

2.

3.

Reflect on the day, remember the positive and acknowledge the lessons.

1 thing I am proud of today and why

_____

_____

_____

_____

1 thing I learned today that I will help me grow

_____

_____

Free Flow Thoughts

Day   Date:

Good morning, today I start the day with gratitude and positive intentions.

How do I feel and how will I show myself some love?

_____

_____

1 thing I am grateful for this morning

_____

_____

I am grateful for this because

_____

_____

3 positive intentions for the day to **show myself love...**

1.

2.

3.

Reflect on the day, remember the positive and acknowledge the lessons.

1 thing I am proud of today and why

_____

_____

_____

_____

1 thing I learned today that I will help me grow

_____

_____

Free Flow Thoughts

Day   Date:

Good morning, today I start the day with gratitude and positive intentions.

How do I feel and how will I show myself some love?

_____

_____

1 thing I am grateful for this morning

_____

_____

I am grateful for this because

_____

_____

3 positive intentions for the day to **show myself love...**

1.

2.

3.

Reflect on the day, remember the positive and acknowledge the lessons.

1 thing I am proud of today and why

_____

_____

_____

_____

1 thing I learned today that I will help me grow

_____

_____

Free Flow Thoughts

Day   Date:

Good morning, today I start the day with gratitude and positive intentions.

How do I feel and how will I show myself some love?

_____

_____

1 thing I am grateful for this morning

_____

_____

I am grateful for this because

_____

_____

3 positive intentions for the day to **show myself love…**

1.

2.

3.

Reflect on the day, remember the positive and acknowledge the lessons.

1 thing I am proud of today and why

_____

_____

_____

_____

1 thing I learned today that I will help me grow

_____

_____

Free Flow Thoughts

Day   Date:

Good morning, today I start the day with gratitude and positive intentions.

How do I feel and how will I show myself some love?

_____

_____

1 thing I am grateful for this morning

_____

_____

I am grateful for this because

_____

_____

3 positive intentions for the day to **show myself love...**

1.

2.

3.

Reflect on the day, remember the positive and acknowledge the lessons.

1 thing I am proud of today and why

_____

_____

_____

_____

1 thing I learned today that I will help me grow

_____

_____

Free Flow Thoughts

Day   Date:

Good morning, today I start the day with gratitude and positive intentions.

How do I feel and how will I show myself some love?

_____

_____

1 thing I am grateful for this morning

_____

_____

I am grateful for this because

_____

_____

3 positive intentions for the day to **show myself love...**

1.

2.

3.

Reflect on the day, remember the positive and acknowledge the lessons.

1 thing I am proud of today and why

_____

_____

_____

_____

1 thing I learned today that I will help me grow

_____

_____

Free Flow Thoughts

Day   Date:

Good morning, today I start the day with gratitude and positive intentions.

How do I feel and how will I show myself some love?

_____

_____

1 thing I am grateful for this morning

_____

_____

I am grateful for this because

_____

_____

3 positive intentions for the day to **show myself love...**

1.

2.

3.

Reflect on the day, remember the positive and acknowledge the lessons.

1 thing I am proud of today and why

_____

_____

_____

1 thing I learned today that I will help me grow

_____

_____

Free Flow Thoughts

Day   Date:

Good morning, today I start the day with gratitude and positive intentions.

How do I feel and how will I show myself some love?

_____

_____

1 thing I am grateful for this morning

_____

_____

I am grateful for this because

_____

_____

3 positive intentions for the day to **show myself love...**

1.

2.

3.

Reflect on the day, remember the positive and acknowledge the lessons.

1 thing I am proud of today and why

_____

_____

_____

_____

1 thing I learned today that I will help me grow

_____

_____

Free Flow Thoughts

Day   Date:

Good morning, today I start the day with gratitude and positive intentions.

How do I feel and how will I show myself some love?

_____

_____

1 thing I am grateful for this morning

_____

_____

I am grateful for this because

_____

_____

3 positive intentions for the day to **show myself love...**

1.

2.

3.

Reflect on the day, remember the positive and acknowledge the lessons.

1 thing I am proud of today and why

_____

_____

_____

_____

1 thing I learned today that I will help me grow

_____

_____

Free Flow Thoughts

Day   Date:

Good morning, today I start the day with gratitude and positive intentions.

How do I feel and how will I show myself some love?

_____

_____

1 thing I am grateful for this morning

_____

_____

I am grateful for this because

_____

_____

3 positive intentions for the day to **show myself love…**

1.

2.

3.

Reflect on the day, remember the positive and acknowledge the lessons.

1 thing I am proud of today and why

_____

_____

_____

_____

1 thing I learned today that I will help me grow

_____

_____

Free Flow Thoughts

Day   Date:

Good morning, today I start the day with gratitude and positive intentions.

How do I feel and how will I show myself some love?

_____

_____

1 thing I am grateful for this morning

_____

_____

I am grateful for this because

_____

_____

3 positive intentions for the day to **show myself love…**

1.

2.

3.

Reflect on the day, remember the positive and acknowledge the lessons.

1 thing I am proud of today and why

_____

_____

_____

_____

1 thing I learned today that I will help me grow

_____

_____

Free Flow Thoughts

Day   Date:

Good morning, today I start the day with gratitude and positive intentions.

How do I feel and how will I show myself some love?

_____

_____

1 thing I am grateful for this morning

_____

_____

I am grateful for this because

_____

_____

3 positive intentions for the day to **show myself love...**

1.

2.

3.

Reflect on the day, remember the positive and acknowledge the lessons.

1 thing I am proud of today and why

_____

_____

_____

_____

1 thing I learned today that I will help me grow

_____

_____

Free Flow Thoughts

Day   Date:

Good morning, today I start the day with gratitude and positive intentions.

How do I feel and how will I show myself some love?

_____

_____

1 thing I am grateful for this morning

_____

_____

I am grateful for this because

_____

_____

3 positive intentions for the day to **show myself love...**

1.

2.

3.

Reflect on the day, remember the positive and acknowledge the lessons.

1 thing I am proud of today and why

_____

_____

_____

_____

1 thing I learned today that I will help me grow

_____

_____

Free Flow Thoughts

Day   Date:

Good morning, today I start the day with gratitude and positive intentions.

How do I feel and how will I show myself some love?

_____

_____

1 thing I am grateful for this morning

_____

_____

I am grateful for this because

_____

_____

3 positive intentions for the day to **show myself love...**

1.

2.

3.

Reflect on the day, remember the positive and acknowledge the lessons.

1 thing I am proud of today and why

_____

_____

_____

_____

1 thing I learned today that I will help me grow

_____

_____

Free Flow Thoughts

Day   Date:

Good morning, today I start the day with gratitude and positive intentions.

How do I feel and how will I show myself some love?

_____

_____

1 thing I am grateful for this morning

_____

_____

I am grateful for this because

_____

_____

3 positive intentions for the day to **show myself love...**

1.

2.

3.

Reflect on the day, remember the positive and acknowledge the lessons.

1 thing I am proud of today and why

_____

_____

_____

_____

1 thing I learned today that I will help me grow

_____

_____

Free Flow Thoughts

Day   Date:

Good morning, today I start the day with gratitude and positive intentions.

How do I feel and how will I show myself some love?

_____

_____

1 thing I am grateful for this morning

_____

_____

I am grateful for this because

_____

_____

3 positive intentions for the day to **show myself love...**

1.

2.

3.

Reflect on the day, remember the positive and acknowledge the lessons.

1 thing I am proud of today and why

_____

_____

_____

_____

1 thing I learned today that I will help me grow

_____

_____

Free Flow Thoughts

Day   Date:

Good morning, today I start the day with gratitude and positive intentions.

How do I feel and how will I show myself some love?

_____

_____

1 thing I am grateful for this morning

_____

_____

I am grateful for this because

_____

_____

3 positive intentions for the day to **show myself love…**

1.

2.

3.

Reflect on the day, remember the positive and acknowledge the lessons.

1 thing I am proud of today and why

_____

_____

_____

_____

1 thing I learned today that I will help me grow

_____

_____

Free Flow Thoughts

Day   Date:

Good morning, today I start the day with gratitude and positive intentions.

How do I feel and how will I show myself some love?

_____

_____

1 thing I am grateful for this morning

_____

_____

I am grateful for this because

_____

_____

3 positive intentions for the day to **show myself love**...

1.

2.

3.

Reflect on the day, remember the positive and acknowledge the lessons.

1 thing I am proud of today and why

_____

_____

_____

_____

1 thing I learned today that I will help me grow

_____

_____

Free Flow Thoughts

Day   Date:

Good morning, today I start the day with gratitude and positive intentions.

How do I feel and how will I show myself some love?

_____

_____

1 thing I am grateful for this morning

_____

_____

I am grateful for this because

_____

_____

3 positive intentions for the day to **show myself love…**

1.

2.

3.

Reflect on the day, remember the positive and acknowledge the lessons.

1 thing I am proud of today and why

_____

_____

_____

_____

1 thing I learned today that I will help me grow

_____

_____

Free Flow Thoughts

Day   Date:

Good morning, today I start the day with gratitude and positive intentions.

How do I feel and how will I show myself some love?

_____

_____

1 thing I am grateful for this morning

_____

_____

I am grateful for this because

_____

_____

3 positive intentions for the day to **show myself love...**

1.

2.

3.

Reflect on the day, remember the positive and acknowledge the lessons.

1 thing I am proud of today and why

_____

_____

_____

_____

1 thing I learned today that I will help me grow

_____

_____

Free Flow Thoughts

Day   Date:

Good morning, today I start the day with gratitude and positive intentions.

How do I feel and how will I show myself some love?

_____

_____

1 thing I am grateful for this morning

_____

_____

I am grateful for this because

_____

_____

3 positive intentions for the day to **show myself love...**

1.

2.

3.

Reflect on the day, remember the positive and acknowledge the lessons.

1 thing I am proud of today and why

_____

_____

_____

_____

1 thing I learned today that I will help me grow

_____

_____

Free Flow Thoughts

Day   Date:

Good morning, today I start the day with gratitude and positive intentions.

How do I feel and how will I show myself some love?

_____

_____

1 thing I am grateful for this morning

_____

_____

I am grateful for this because

_____

_____

3 positive intentions for the day to **show myself love...**

1.

2.

3.

Reflect on the day, remember the positive and acknowledge the lessons.

1 thing I am proud of today and why

_____

_____

_____

1 thing I learned today that I will help me grow

_____

_____

Free Flow Thoughts

Day   Date:

Good morning, today I start the day with gratitude and positive intentions.

How do I feel and how will I show myself some love?

_____

_____

1 thing I am grateful for this morning

_____

_____

I am grateful for this because

_____

_____

3 positive intentions for the day to **show myself love...**

1.

2.

3.

Reflect on the day, remember the positive and acknowledge the lessons.

1 thing I am proud of today and why

_____

_____

_____

_____

1 thing I learned today that I will help me grow

_____

_____

Free Flow Thoughts

Day   Date:

Good morning, today I start the day with gratitude and positive intentions.

How do I feel and how will I show myself some love?

_____

_____

1 thing I am grateful for this morning

_____

_____

I am grateful for this because

_____

_____

3 positive intentions for the day to **show myself love...**

1.

2.

3.

Reflect on the day, remember the positive and acknowledge the lessons.

1 thing I am proud of today and why

_____

_____

_____

_____

1 thing I learned today that I will help me grow

_____

_____

Free Flow Thoughts

Day   Date:

Good morning, today I start the day with gratitude and positive intentions.

How do I feel and how will I show myself some love?

_____

_____

1 thing I am grateful for this morning

_____

_____

I am grateful for this because

_____

_____

3 positive intentions for the day to **show myself love...**

1.

2.

3.

Reflect on the day, remember the positive and acknowledge the lessons.

1 thing I am proud of today and why

_____

_____

_____

_____

1 thing I learned today that I will help me grow

_____

_____

Free Flow Thoughts

Day   Date:

Good morning, today I start the day with gratitude and positive intentions.

How do I feel and how will I show myself some love?

_____

_____

1 thing I am grateful for this morning

_____

_____

I am grateful for this because

_____

_____

3 positive intentions for the day to **show myself love...**

1.

2.

3.

Reflect on the day, remember the positive and acknowledge the lessons.

1 thing I am proud of today and why

_____

_____

_____

_____

1 thing I learned today that I will help me grow

_____

_____

Free Flow Thoughts

Day   Date:

Good morning, today I start the day with gratitude and positive intentions.

How do I feel and how will I show myself some love?

_____

_____

1 thing I am grateful for this morning

_____

_____

I am grateful for this because

_____

_____

3 positive intentions for the day to **show myself love...**

1.

2.

3.

Reflect on the day, remember the positive and acknowledge the lessons.

1 thing I am proud of today and why

_____

_____

_____

_____

1 thing I learned today that I will help me grow

_____

_____

Free Flow Thoughts

Day   Date:

Good morning, today I start the day with gratitude and positive intentions.

How do I feel and how will I show myself some love?

_____

_____

1 thing I am grateful for this morning

_____

_____

I am grateful for this because

_____

_____

3 positive intentions for the day to **show myself love…**

1.

2.

3.

Reflect on the day, remember the positive and acknowledge the lessons.

1 thing I am proud of today and why

_____

_____

_____

_____

1 thing I learned today that I will help me grow

_____

_____

Free Flow Thoughts

Day   Date:

Good morning, today I start the day with gratitude and positive intentions.

How do I feel and how will I show myself some love?

_____

_____

1 thing I am grateful for this morning

_____

_____

I am grateful for this because

_____

_____

3 positive intentions for the day to **show myself love...**

1.

2.

3.

Reflect on the day, remember the positive and acknowledge the lessons.

1 thing I am proud of today and why

_____

_____

_____

_____

1 thing I learned today that I will help me grow

_____

_____

Free Flow Thoughts

Day   Date:

Good morning, today I start the day with gratitude and positive intentions.

How do I feel and how will I show myself some love?

_____

_____

1 thing I am grateful for this morning

_____

_____

I am grateful for this because

_____

_____

3 positive intentions for the day to **show myself love...**

1.

2.

3.

Reflect on the day, remember the positive and acknowledge the lessons.

1 thing I am proud of today and why

_____

_____

_____

_____

1 thing I learned today that I will help me grow

_____

_____

Free Flow Thoughts

Day   Date:

Good morning, today I start the day with gratitude and positive intentions.

How do I feel and how will I show myself some love?

_____

_____

1 thing I am grateful for this morning

_____

_____

I am grateful for this because

_____

_____

3 positive intentions for the day to **show myself love...**

1.

2.

3.

Reflect on the day, remember the positive and acknowledge the lessons.

1 thing I am proud of today and why

_____

_____

_____

_____

1 thing I learned today that I will help me grow

_____

_____

Free Flow Thoughts

Day   Date:

Good morning, today I start the day with gratitude and positive intentions.

How do I feel and how will I show myself some love?

_____

_____

1 thing I am grateful for this morning

_____

_____

I am grateful for this because

_____

_____

3 positive intentions for the day to **show myself love...**

1.

2.

3.

Reflect on the day, remember the positive and acknowledge the lessons.

1 thing I am proud of today and why

_____

_____

_____

_____

1 thing I learned today that I will help me grow

_____

_____

Free Flow Thoughts

Day   Date:

Good morning, today I start the day with gratitude and positive intentions.

How do I feel and how will I show myself some love?

_____

_____

1 thing I am grateful for this morning

_____

_____

I am grateful for this because

_____

_____

3 positive intentions for the day to **show myself love...**

1.

2.

3.

Reflect on the day, remember the positive and acknowledge the lessons.

1 thing I am proud of today and why

_____

_____

_____

_____

1 thing I learned today that I will help me grow

_____

_____

Free Flow Thoughts

Day   Date:

Good morning, today I start the day with gratitude and positive intentions.

How do I feel and how will I show myself some love?

_____

_____

1 thing I am grateful for this morning

_____

_____

I am grateful for this because

_____

_____

3 positive intentions for the day to **show myself love...**

1.

2.

3.

Reflect on the day, remember the positive and acknowledge the lessons.

1 thing I am proud of today and why

_____

_____

_____

_____

1 thing I learned today that I will help me grow

_____

_____

Free Flow Thoughts

Day   Date:

Good morning, today I start the day with gratitude and positive intentions.

How do I feel and how will I show myself some love?

_____

_____

1 thing I am grateful for this morning

_____

_____

I am grateful for this because

_____

_____

3 positive intentions for the day to **show myself love...**

1.

2.

3.

Reflect on the day, remember the positive and acknowledge the lessons.

1 thing I am proud of today and why

_____

_____

_____

_____

1 thing I learned today that I will help me grow

_____

_____

… Free Flow Thoughts

Day   Date:

Good morning, today I start the day with gratitude and positive intentions.

How do I feel and how will I show myself some love?

_____

_____

1 thing I am grateful for this morning

_____

_____

I am grateful for this because

_____

_____

3 positive intentions for the day to **show myself love…**

1.

2.

3.

Reflect on the day, remember the positive and acknowledge the lessons.

1 thing I am proud of today and why

_____

_____

_____

_____

1 thing I learned today that I will help me grow

_____

_____

Free Flow Thoughts

Day   Date:

Good morning, today I start the day with gratitude and positive intentions.

How do I feel and how will I show myself some love?

_____

_____

1 thing I am grateful for this morning

_____

_____

I am grateful for this because

_____

_____

3 positive intentions for the day to **show myself love...**

1.

2.

3.

Reflect on the day, remember the positive and acknowledge the lessons.

1 thing I am proud of today and why

_____

_____

_____

1 thing I learned today that I will help me grow

_____

_____

Free Flow Thoughts

Day   Date:

Good morning, today I start the day with gratitude and positive intentions.

How do I feel and how will I show myself some love?

_____

_____

1 thing I am grateful for this morning

_____

_____

I am grateful for this because

_____

_____

3 positive intentions for the day to **show myself love…**

1.

2.

3.

Reflect on the day, remember the positive and acknowledge the lessons.

1 thing I am proud of today and why

_____

_____

_____

_____

1 thing I learned today that I will help me grow

_____

_____

Free Flow Thoughts

Day   Date:

Good morning, today I start the day with gratitude and positive intentions.

How do I feel and how will I show myself some love?

_____

_____

1 thing I am grateful for this morning

_____

_____

I am grateful for this because

_____

_____

3 positive intentions for the day to **show myself love...**

1.

2.

3.

Reflect on the day, remember the positive and acknowledge the lessons.

1 thing I am proud of today and why

_____

_____

_____

_____

1 thing I learned today that I will help me grow

_____

_____

Free Flow Thoughts

Day   Date:

Good morning, today I start the day with gratitude and positive intentions.

How do I feel and how will I show myself some love?

_____

_____

1 thing I am grateful for this morning

_____

_____

I am grateful for this because

_____

_____

3 positive intentions for the day to **show myself love...**

1.

2.

3.

Reflect on the day, remember the positive and acknowledge the lessons.

1 thing I am proud of today and why

_____

_____

_____

_____

1 thing I learned today that I will help me grow

_____

_____

Free Flow Thoughts

Day   Date:

Good morning, today I start the day with gratitude and positive intentions.

How do I feel and how will I show myself some love?

_____

_____

1 thing I am grateful for this morning

_____

_____

I am grateful for this because

_____

_____

3 positive intentions for the day to **show myself love…**

1.

2.

3.

Reflect on the day, remember the positive and acknowledge the lessons.

1 thing I am proud of today and why

_____

_____

_____

_____

1 thing I learned today that I will help me grow

_____

_____

Free Flow Thoughts

Day   Date:

Good morning, today I start the day with gratitude and positive intentions.

How do I feel and how will I show myself some love?

_____

_____

1 thing I am grateful for this morning

_____

_____

I am grateful for this because

_____

_____

3 positive intentions for the day to **show myself love...**

1.

2.

3.

Reflect on the day, remember the positive and acknowledge the lessons.

1 thing I am proud of today and why

_____

_____

_____

_____

1 thing I learned today that I will help me grow

_____

_____

Free Flow Thoughts

Day   Date:

Good morning, today I start the day with gratitude and positive intentions.

How do I feel and how will I show myself some love?

_____

_____

1 thing I am grateful for this morning

_____

_____

I am grateful for this because

_____

_____

3 positive intentions for the day to **show myself love...**

1.

2.

3.

Reflect on the day, remember the positive and acknowledge the lessons.

1 thing I am proud of today and why

_____

_____

_____

_____

1 thing I learned today that I will help me grow

_____

_____

Free Flow Thoughts

Day   Date:

Good morning, today I start the day with gratitude and positive intentions.

How do I feel and how will I show myself some love?

_____

_____

1 thing I am grateful for this morning

_____

_____

I am grateful for this because

_____

_____

3 positive intentions for the day to **show myself love…**

1.

2.

3.

Reflect on the day, remember the positive and acknowledge the lessons.

1 thing I am proud of today and why

_____

_____

_____

_____

1 thing I learned today that I will help me grow

_____

_____

Free Flow Thoughts

Day   Date:

Good morning, today I start the day with gratitude and positive intentions.

How do I feel and how will I show myself some love?

_____

_____

1 thing I am grateful for this morning

_____

_____

I am grateful for this because

_____

_____

3 positive intentions for the day to **show myself love...**

1.

2.

3.

Reflect on the day, remember the positive and acknowledge the lessons.

1 thing I am proud of today and why

_____

_____

_____

_____

1 thing I learned today that I will help me grow

_____

_____

Free Flow Thoughts

Day   Date:

Good morning, today I start the day with gratitude and positive intentions.

How do I feel and how will I show myself some love?

_____

_____

1 thing I am grateful for this morning

_____

_____

I am grateful for this because

_____

_____

3 positive intentions for the day to **show myself love...**

1.

2.

3.

Reflect on the day, remember the positive and acknowledge the lessons.

1 thing I am proud of today and why

_____

_____

_____

_____

1 thing I learned today that I will help me grow

_____

_____

Free Flow Thoughts

Day   Date:

Good morning, today I start the day with gratitude and positive intentions.

How do I feel and how will I show myself some love?

_____

_____

1 thing I am grateful for this morning

_____

_____

I am grateful for this because

_____

_____

3 positive intentions for the day to **show myself love...**

1.

2.

3.

Reflect on the day, remember the positive and acknowledge the lessons.

1 thing I am proud of today and why

_____

_____

_____

_____

1 thing I learned today that I will help me grow

_____

_____

Free Flow Thoughts

Day   Date:

Good morning, today I start the day with gratitude and positive intentions.

How do I feel and how will I show myself some love?

_____

_____

1 thing I am grateful for this morning

_____

_____

I am grateful for this because

_____

_____

3 positive intentions for the day to **show myself love…**

1.

2.

3.

Reflect on the day, remember the positive and acknowledge the lessons.

1 thing I am proud of today and why

_____

_____

_____

_____

1 thing I learned today that I will help me grow

_____

_____

Free Flow Thoughts

Day   Date:

Good morning, today I start the day with gratitude and positive intentions.

How do I feel and how will I show myself some love?

_____

_____

1 thing I am grateful for this morning

_____

_____

I am grateful for this because

_____

_____

3 positive intentions for the day to **show myself love...**

1.

2.

3.

Reflect on the day, remember the positive and acknowledge the lessons.

1 thing I am proud of today and why

_____

_____

_____

_____

1 thing I learned today that I will help me grow

_____

_____

Free Flow Thoughts

Day   Date:

Good morning, today I start the day with gratitude and positive intentions.

How do I feel and how will I show myself some love?

_____

_____

1 thing I am grateful for this morning

_____

_____

I am grateful for this because

_____

_____

3 positive intentions for the day to **show myself love...**

1.

2.

3.

Reflect on the day, remember the positive and acknowledge the lessons.

1 thing I am proud of today and why

_____

_____

_____

_____

1 thing I learned today that I will help me grow

_____

_____

Free Flow Thoughts

Day   Date:

Good morning, today I start the day with gratitude and positive intentions.

How do I feel and how will I show myself some love?

_____

_____

1 thing I am grateful for this morning

_____

_____

I am grateful for this because

_____

_____

3 positive intentions for the day to **show myself love...**

1.

2.

3.

Reflect on the day, remember the positive and acknowledge the lessons.

1 thing I am proud of today and why

_____

_____

_____

_____

1 thing I learned today that I will help me grow

_____

_____

Free Flow Thoughts

Day   Date:

Good morning, today I start the day with gratitude and positive intentions.

How do I feel and how will I show myself some love?

_____

_____

1 thing I am grateful for this morning

_____

_____

I am grateful for this because

_____

_____

3 positive intentions for the day to **show myself love…**

1.

2.

3.

Reflect on the day, remember the positive and acknowledge the lessons.

1 thing I am proud of today and why

_____

_____

_____

_____

1 thing I learned today that I will help me grow

_____

_____

Free Flow Thoughts

Day   Date:

Good morning, today I start the day with gratitude and positive intentions.

How do I feel and how will I show myself some love?

_____

_____

1 thing I am grateful for this morning

_____

_____

I am grateful for this because

_____

_____

3 positive intentions for the day to **show myself love…**

1.

2.

3.

Reflect on the day, remember the positive and acknowledge the lessons.

1 thing I am proud of today and why

_____

_____

_____

_____

1 thing I learned today that I will help me grow

_____

_____

Free Flow Thoughts

Day   Date:

Good morning, today I start the day with gratitude and positive intentions.

How do I feel and how will I show myself some love?

_____

_____

1 thing I am grateful for this morning

_____

_____

I am grateful for this because

_____

_____

3 positive intentions for the day to **show myself love...**

1.

2.

3.

Reflect on the day, remember the positive and acknowledge the lessons.

1 thing I am proud of today and why

_____

_____

_____

_____

1 thing I learned today that I will help me grow

_____

_____

Free Flow Thoughts

Day   Date:

Good morning, today I start the day with gratitude and positive intentions.

How do I feel and how will I show myself some love?

_____

_____

1 thing I am grateful for this morning

_____

_____

I am grateful for this because

_____

_____

3 positive intentions for the day to **show myself love...**

1.

2.

3.

Reflect on the day, remember the positive and acknowledge the lessons.

1 thing I am proud of today and why

_____

_____

_____

_____

1 thing I learned today that I will help me grow

_____

_____

Free Flow Thoughts

Day   Date:

Good morning, today I start the day with gratitude and positive intentions.

How do I feel and how will I show myself some love?

_____

_____

1 thing I am grateful for this morning

_____

_____

I am grateful for this because

_____

_____

3 positive intentions for the day to **show myself love…**

1.

2.

3.

Reflect on the day, remember the positive and acknowledge the lessons.

1 thing I am proud of today and why

_____

_____

_____

_____

1 thing I learned today that I will help me grow

_____

_____

Free Flow Thoughts

Day   Date:

Good morning, today I start the day with gratitude and positive intentions.

How do I feel and how will I show myself some love?

_____

_____

1 thing I am grateful for this morning

_____

_____

I am grateful for this because

_____

_____

3 positive intentions for the day to **show myself love...**

1.

2.

3.

Reflect on the day, remember the positive and acknowledge the lessons.

1 thing I am proud of today and why

_____

_____

_____

_____

1 thing I learned today that I will help me grow

_____

_____

Free Flow Thoughts

Day   Date:

Good morning, today I start the day with gratitude and positive intentions.

How do I feel and how will I show myself some love?

_____

_____

1 thing I am grateful for this morning

_____

_____

I am grateful for this because

_____

_____

3 positive intentions for the day to **show myself love…**

1.

2.

3.

Reflect on the day, remember the positive and acknowledge the lessons.

1 thing I am proud of today and why

_____

_____

_____

1 thing I learned today that I will help me grow

_____

_____

Free Flow Thoughts

Day   Date:

Good morning, today I start the day with gratitude and positive intentions.

How do I feel and how will I show myself some love?

_____

_____

1 thing I am grateful for this morning

_____

_____

I am grateful for this because

_____

_____

3 positive intentions for the day to **show myself love...**

1.

2.

3.

Reflect on the day, remember the positive and acknowledge the lessons.

1 thing I am proud of today and why

_____

_____

_____

_____

1 thing I learned today that I will help me grow

_____

_____

Free Flow Thoughts

Day   Date:

Good morning, today I start the day with gratitude and positive intentions.

How do I feel and how will I show myself some love?

_____

_____

1 thing I am grateful for this morning

_____

_____

I am grateful for this because

_____

_____

3 positive intentions for the day to **show myself love...**

1.

2.

3.

Reflect on the day, remember the positive and acknowledge the lessons.

1 thing I am proud of today and why

_____

_____

_____

_____

1 thing I learned today that I will help me grow

_____

_____

Free Flow Thoughts

Day   Date:

Good morning, today I start the day with gratitude and positive intentions.

How do I feel and how will I show myself some love?

_____

_____

1 thing I am grateful for this morning

_____

_____

I am grateful for this because

_____

_____

3 positive intentions for the day to **show myself love…**

1.

2.

3.

Reflect on the day, remember the positive and acknowledge the lessons.

1 thing I am proud of today and why

_____

_____

_____

_____

1 thing I learned today that I will help me grow

_____

_____

Free Flow Thoughts

Day   Date:

Good morning, today I start the day with gratitude and positive intentions.

How do I feel and how will I show myself some love?

_____

_____

1 thing I am grateful for this morning

_____

_____

I am grateful for this because

_____

_____

3 positive intentions for the day to **show myself love...**

1.

2.

3.

Reflect on the day, remember the positive and acknowledge the lessons.

1 thing I am proud of today and why

_____

_____

_____

_____

1 thing I learned today that I will help me grow

_____

_____

Free Flow Thoughts

Day   Date:

Good morning, today I start the day with gratitude and positive intentions.

How do I feel and how will I show myself some love?

_____

_____

1 thing I am grateful for this morning

_____

_____

I am grateful for this because

_____

_____

3 positive intentions for the day to **show myself love...**

1.

2.

3.

Reflect on the day, remember the positive and acknowledge the lessons.

1 thing I am proud of today and why

_____

_____

_____

_____

1 thing I learned today that I will help me grow

_____

_____

Free Flow Thoughts

Day   Date:

Good morning, today I start the day with gratitude and positive intentions.

How do I feel and how will I show myself some love?

_____

_____

1 thing I am grateful for this morning

_____

_____

I am grateful for this because

_____

_____

3 positive intentions for the day to **show myself love...**

1.

2.

3.

Reflect on the day, remember the positive and acknowledge the lessons.

1 thing I am proud of today and why

_____

_____

_____

1 thing I learned today that I will help me grow

_____

_____

Free Flow Thoughts

Day   Date:

Good morning, today I start the day with gratitude and positive intentions.

How do I feel and how will I show myself some love?

_____
_____

1 thing I am grateful for this morning

_____
_____

I am grateful for this because

_____
_____

3 positive intentions for the day to **show myself love…**

1.

2.

3.

Reflect on the day, remember the positive and acknowledge the lessons.

1 thing I am proud of today and why

_____
_____
_____
_____

1 thing I learned today that I will help me grow

_____
_____

Free Flow Thoughts

Day   Date:

Good morning, today I start the day with gratitude and positive intentions.

How do I feel and how will I show myself some love?

_____

_____

1 thing I am grateful for this morning

_____

_____

I am grateful for this because

_____

_____

3 positive intentions for the day to **show myself love...**

1.

2.

3.

Reflect on the day, remember the positive and acknowledge the lessons.

1 thing I am proud of today and why

_____

_____

_____

_____

1 thing I learned today that I will help me grow

_____

_____

Free Flow Thoughts

Day   Date:

Good morning, today I start the day with gratitude and positive intentions.

How do I feel and how will I show myself some love?

_____

_____

1 thing I am grateful for this morning

_____

_____

I am grateful for this because

_____

_____

3 positive intentions for the day to **show myself love…**

1.

2.

3.

Reflect on the day, remember the positive and acknowledge the lessons.

1 thing I am proud of today and why

_____

_____

_____

_____

1 thing I learned today that I will help me grow

_____

_____

Free Flow Thoughts

Day   Date:

Good morning, today I start the day with gratitude and positive intentions.

How do I feel and how will I show myself some love?

_____

_____

1 thing I am grateful for this morning

_____

_____

I am grateful for this because

_____

_____

3 positive intentions for the day to **show myself love...**

1.

2.

3.

Reflect on the day, remember the positive and acknowledge the lessons.

1 thing I am proud of today and why

_____

_____

_____

_____

1 thing I learned today that I will help me grow

_____

_____

Free Flow Thoughts

Day   Date:

Good morning, today I start the day with gratitude and positive intentions.

How do I feel and how will I show myself some love?

_____

_____

1 thing I am grateful for this morning

_____

_____

I am grateful for this because

_____

_____

3 positive intentions for the day to **show myself love...**

1.

2.

3.

Reflect on the day, remember the positive and acknowledge the lessons.

1 thing I am proud of today and why

_____

_____

_____

_____

1 thing I learned today that I will help me grow

_____

_____

Free Flow Thoughts

Day   Date:

Good morning, today I start the day with gratitude and positive intentions.

How do I feel and how will I show myself some love?

_____

_____

1 thing I am grateful for this morning

_____

_____

I am grateful for this because

_____

_____

3 positive intentions for the day to **show myself love...**

1.

2.

3.

Reflect on the day, remember the positive and acknowledge the lessons.

1 thing I am proud of today and why

_____

_____

_____

_____

1 thing I learned today that I will help me grow

_____

_____

Free Flow Thoughts

Day   Date:

Good morning, today I start the day with gratitude and positive intentions.

How do I feel and how will I show myself some love?

_____

_____

1 thing I am grateful for this morning

_____

_____

I am grateful for this because

_____

_____

3 positive intentions for the day to **show myself love…**

1.

2.

3.

Reflect on the day, remember the positive and acknowledge the lessons.

1 thing I am proud of today and why

_____

_____

_____

_____

1 thing I learned today that I will help me grow

_____

_____

Free Flow Thoughts

Day   Date:

Good morning, today I start the day with gratitude and positive intentions.

How do I feel and how will I show myself some love?

_____

_____

1 thing I am grateful for this morning

_____

_____

I am grateful for this because

_____

_____

3 positive intentions for the day to **show myself love...**

1.

2.

3.

Reflect on the day, remember the positive and acknowledge the lessons.

1 thing I am proud of today and why

_____

_____

_____

_____

1 thing I learned today that I will help me grow

_____

_____

Free Flow Thoughts

Day   Date:

Good morning, today I start the day with gratitude and positive intentions.

How do I feel and how will I show myself some love?

_____

_____

1 thing I am grateful for this morning

_____

_____

I am grateful for this because

_____

_____

3 positive intentions for the day to **show myself love...**

1.

2.

3.

Reflect on the day, remember the positive and acknowledge the lessons.

1 thing I am proud of today and why

_____

_____

_____

_____

1 thing I learned today that I will help me grow

_____

_____

Free Flow Thoughts

Day   Date:

Good morning, today I start the day with gratitude and positive intentions.

How do I feel and how will I show myself some love?

_____

_____

1 thing I am grateful for this morning

_____

_____

I am grateful for this because

_____

_____

3 positive intentions for the day to **show myself love...**

1.

2.

3.

Reflect on the day, remember the positive and acknowledge the lessons.

1 thing I am proud of today and why

_____

_____

_____

_____

1 thing I learned today that I will help me grow

_____

_____

Free Flow Thoughts

Day   Date:

Good morning, today I start the day with gratitude and positive intentions.

How do I feel and how will I show myself some love?

_____

_____

1 thing I am grateful for this morning

_____

_____

I am grateful for this because

_____

_____

3 positive intentions for the day to **show myself love...**

1.

2.

3.

Reflect on the day, remember the positive and acknowledge the lessons.

1 thing I am proud of today and why

_____

_____

_____

_____

1 thing I learned today that I will help me grow

_____

_____

Free Flow Thoughts

Day   Date:

Good morning, today I start the day with gratitude and positive intentions.

How do I feel and how will I show myself some love?

_____

_____

1 thing I am grateful for this morning

_____

_____

I am grateful for this because

_____

_____

3 positive intentions for the day to **show myself love…**

1.

2.

3.

Reflect on the day, remember the positive and acknowledge the lessons.

1 thing I am proud of today and why

_____

_____

_____

1 thing I learned today that I will help me grow

_____

_____

Free Flow Thoughts

Day   Date:

Good morning, today I start the day with gratitude and positive intentions.

How do I feel and how will I show myself some love?

_____

_____

1 thing I am grateful for this morning

_____

_____

I am grateful for this because

_____

_____

3 positive intentions for the day to **show myself love...**

1.

2.

3.

Reflect on the day, remember the positive and acknowledge the lessons.

1 thing I am proud of today and why

_____

_____

_____

_____

1 thing I learned today that I will help me grow

_____

_____

Free Flow Thoughts

Day   Date:

Good morning, today I start the day with gratitude and positive intentions.

How do I feel and how will I show myself some love?

_____

_____

1 thing I am grateful for this morning

_____

_____

I am grateful for this because

_____

_____

3 positive intentions for the day to **show myself love...**

1.

2.

3.

Reflect on the day, remember the positive and acknowledge the lessons.

1 thing I am proud of today and why

_____

_____

_____

_____

1 thing I learned today that I will help me grow

_____

_____

Free Flow Thoughts

Day   Date:

Good morning, today I start the day with gratitude and positive intentions.

How do I feel and how will I show myself some love?

_____

_____

1 thing I am grateful for this morning

_____

_____

I am grateful for this because

_____

_____

3 positive intentions for the day to **show myself love...**

1.

2.

3.

Reflect on the day, remember the positive and acknowledge the lessons.

1 thing I am proud of today and why

_____

_____

_____

_____

1 thing I learned today that I will help me grow

_____

_____

Free Flow Thoughts

Day   Date:

Good morning, today I start the day with gratitude and positive intentions.

How do I feel and how will I show myself some love?

_____
_____

1 thing I am grateful for this morning

_____
_____

I am grateful for this because

_____
_____

3 positive intentions for the day to **show myself love…**

1.

2.

3.

Reflect on the day, remember the positive and acknowledge the lessons.

1 thing I am proud of today and why

_____
_____
_____
_____

1 thing I learned today that I will help me grow

_____
_____

Free Flow Thoughts

Day   Date:

Good morning, today I start the day with gratitude and positive intentions.

How do I feel and how will I show myself some love?

_____

_____

1 thing I am grateful for this morning

_____

_____

I am grateful for this because

_____

_____

3 positive intentions for the day to **show myself love...**

1.

2.

3.

Reflect on the day, remember the positive and acknowledge the lessons.

1 thing I am proud of today and why

_____

_____

_____

_____

1 thing I learned today that I will help me grow

_____

_____

Free Flow Thoughts

Day   Date:

Good morning, today I start the day with gratitude and positive intentions.

How do I feel and how will I show myself some love?

_____

_____

1 thing I am grateful for this morning

_____

_____

I am grateful for this because

_____

_____

3 positive intentions for the day to **show myself love...**

1.

2.

3.

Reflect on the day, remember the positive and acknowledge the lessons.

1 thing I am proud of today and why

_____

_____

_____

_____

1 thing I learned today that I will help me grow

_____

_____

Free Flow Thoughts

Day   Date:

Good morning, today I start the day with gratitude and positive intentions.

How do I feel and how will I show myself some love?

_____

_____

1 thing I am grateful for this morning

_____

_____

I am grateful for this because

_____

_____

3 positive intentions for the day to **show myself love...**

1.

2.

3.

Reflect on the day, remember the positive and acknowledge the lessons.

1 thing I am proud of today and why

_____

_____

_____

_____

1 thing I learned today that I will help me grow

_____

_____

Free Flow Thoughts Day

Date:

Good morning, today I start the day with gratitude and positive intentions.

How do I feel and how will I show myself some love?

_____

_____

1 thing I am grateful for this morning

_____

_____

I am grateful for this because

_____

_____

3 positive intentions for the day to **show myself love...**

1.

2.

3.

Reflect on the day, remember the positive and acknowledge the lessons.

1 thing I am proud of today and why

_____

_____

_____

_____

1 thing I learned today that I will help me grow

_____

_____

Free Flow Thoughts

Day   Date:

Good morning, today I start the day with gratitude and positive intentions.

How do I feel and how will I show myself some love?

_____

_____

1 thing I am grateful for this morning

_____

_____

I am grateful for this because

_____

_____

3 positive intentions for the day to **show myself love...**

1.

2.

3.

Reflect on the day, remember the positive and acknowledge the lessons.

1 thing I am proud of today and why

_____

_____

_____

_____

1 thing I learned today that I will help me grow

_____

_____

Free Flow Thoughts

Day   Date:

Good morning, today I start the day with gratitude and positive intentions.

How do I feel and how will I show myself some love?

_____

_____

1 thing I am grateful for this morning

_____

_____

I am grateful for this because

_____

_____

3 positive intentions for the day to **show myself love...**

1.

2.

3.

Reflect on the day, remember the positive and acknowledge the lessons.

1 thing I am proud of today and why

_____

_____

_____

_____

1 thing I learned today that I will help me grow

_____

_____

Free Flow Thoughts

Day   Date:

Good morning, today I start the day with gratitude and positive intentions.

How do I feel and how will I show myself some love?

_____
_____

1 thing I am grateful for this morning

_____
_____

I am grateful for this because

_____
_____

3 positive intentions for the day to **show myself love...**

1.

2.

3.

Reflect on the day, remember the positive and acknowledge the lessons.

1 thing I am proud of today and why

_____
_____
_____
_____

1 thing I learned today that I will help me grow

_____
_____

Free Flow Thoughts

Day   Date:

Good morning, today I start the day with gratitude and positive intentions.

How do I feel and how will I show myself some love?

_____

_____

1 thing I am grateful for this morning

_____

_____

I am grateful for this because

_____

_____

3 positive intentions for the day to **show myself love...**

1.

2.

3.

Reflect on the day, remember the positive and acknowledge the lessons.

1 thing I am proud of today and why

_____

_____

_____

_____

1 thing I learned today that I will help me grow

_____

_____

Free Flow Thoughts

Day   Date:

Good morning, today I start the day with gratitude and positive intentions.

How do I feel and how will I show myself some love?

_____

_____

1 thing I am grateful for this morning

_____

_____

I am grateful for this because

_____

_____

3 positive intentions for the day to **show myself love…**

1.

2.

3.

Reflect on the day, remember the positive and acknowledge the lessons.

1 thing I am proud of today and why

_____

_____

_____

_____

1 thing I learned today that I will help me grow

_____

_____

Free Flow Thoughts

Day   Date:

Good morning, today I start the day with gratitude and positive intentions.

How do I feel and how will I show myself some love?

_____

_____

1 thing I am grateful for this morning

_____

_____

I am grateful for this because

_____

_____

3 positive intentions for the day to **show myself love...**

1.

2.

3.

Reflect on the day, remember the positive and acknowledge the lessons.

1 thing I am proud of today and why

_____

_____

_____

_____

1 thing I learned today that I will help me grow

_____

_____

Free Flow Thoughts

Day   Date:

Good morning, today I start the day with gratitude and positive intentions.

How do I feel and how will I show myself some love?

_____

_____

1 thing I am grateful for this morning

_____

_____

I am grateful for this because

_____

_____

3 positive intentions for the day to **show myself love...**

1.

2.

3.

Reflect on the day, remember the positive and acknowledge the lessons.

1 thing I am proud of today and why

_____

_____

_____

_____

1 thing I learned today that I will help me grow

_____

_____

Free Flow Thoughts

Day   Date:

Good morning, today I start the day with gratitude and positive intentions.

How do I feel and how will I show myself some love?

_____

_____

1 thing I am grateful for this morning

_____

_____

I am grateful for this because

_____

_____

3 positive intentions for the day to **show myself love…**

1.

2.

3.

Reflect on the day, remember the positive and acknowledge the lessons.

1 thing I am proud of today and why

_____

_____

_____

_____

1 thing I learned today that I will help me grow

_____

_____

Free Flow Thoughts

Day   Date:

Good morning, today I start the day with gratitude and positive intentions.

How do I feel and how will I show myself some love?

_____
_____

1 thing I am grateful for this morning

_____
_____

I am grateful for this because

_____
_____

3 positive intentions for the day to **show myself love...**

1.

2.

3.

Reflect on the day, remember the positive and acknowledge the lessons.

1 thing I am proud of today and why

_____
_____
_____
_____

1 thing I learned today that I will help me grow

_____
_____

Free Flow Thoughts

Day   Date:

Good morning, today I start the day with gratitude and positive intentions.

How do I feel and how will I show myself some love?

_____

_____

1 thing I am grateful for this morning

_____

_____

I am grateful for this because

_____

_____

3 positive intentions for the day to **show myself love...**

1.

2.

3.

Reflect on the day, remember the positive and acknowledge the lessons.

1 thing I am proud of today and why

_____

_____

_____

_____

1 thing I learned today that I will help me grow

_____

_____

… Free Flow Thoughts

Day   Date:

Good morning, today I start the day with gratitude and positive intentions.

How do I feel and how will I show myself some love?

_____

_____

1 thing I am grateful for this morning

_____

_____

I am grateful for this because

_____

_____

3 positive intentions for the day to **show myself love...**

1.

2.

3.

Reflect on the day, remember the positive and acknowledge the lessons.

1 thing I am proud of today and why

_____

_____

_____

_____

1 thing I learned today that I will help me grow

_____

_____

Free Flow Thoughts

Day   Date:

Good morning, today I start the day with gratitude and positive intentions.

How do I feel and how will I show myself some love?

_____

_____

1 thing I am grateful for this morning

_____

_____

I am grateful for this because

_____

_____

3 positive intentions for the day to **show myself love...**

1.

2.

3.

Reflect on the day, remember the positive and acknowledge the lessons.

1 thing I am proud of today and why

_____

_____

_____

_____

1 thing I learned today that I will help me grow

_____

_____

Free Flow Thoughts

Day   Date:

Good morning, today I start the day with gratitude and positive intentions.

How do I feel and how will I show myself some love?

_____

_____

1 thing I am grateful for this morning

_____

_____

I am grateful for this because

_____

_____

3 positive intentions for the day to **show myself love...**

1.

2.

3.

Reflect on the day, remember the positive and acknowledge the lessons.

1 thing I am proud of today and why

_____

_____

_____

_____

1 thing I learned today that I will help me grow

_____

_____

Free Flow Thoughts

Day   Date:

Good morning, today I start the day with gratitude and positive intentions.

How do I feel and how will I show myself some love?

_____

_____

1 thing I am grateful for this morning

_____

_____

I am grateful for this because

_____

_____

3 positive intentions for the day to **show myself love...**

1.

2.

3.

Reflect on the day, remember the positive and acknowledge the lessons.

1 thing I am proud of today and why

_____

_____

_____

_____

1 thing I learned today that I will help me grow

_____

_____

Free Flow Thoughts

Day   Date:

Good morning, today I start the day with gratitude and positive intentions.

How do I feel and how will I show myself some love?

_____

_____

1 thing I am grateful for this morning

_____

_____

I am grateful for this because

_____

_____

3 positive intentions for the day to **show myself love...**

1.

2.

3.

Reflect on the day, remember the positive and acknowledge the lessons.

1 thing I am proud of today and why

_____

_____

_____

_____

1 thing I learned today that I will help me grow

_____

_____

Free Flow Thoughts

Day   Date:

Good morning, today I start the day with gratitude and positive intentions.

How do I feel and how will I show myself some love?

_____

_____

1 thing I am grateful for this morning

_____

_____

I am grateful for this because

_____

_____

3 positive intentions for the day to **show myself love...**

1.

2.

3.

Reflect on the day, remember the positive and acknowledge the lessons.

1 thing I am proud of today and why

_____

_____

_____

_____

1 thing I learned today that I will help me grow

_____

_____

Free Flow Thoughts

Day   Date:

Good morning, today I start the day with gratitude and positive intentions.

How do I feel and how will I show myself some love?

_____

_____

1 thing I am grateful for this morning

_____

_____

I am grateful for this because

_____

_____

3 positive intentions for the day to **show myself love...**

1.

2.

3.

Reflect on the day, remember the positive and acknowledge the lessons.

1 thing I am proud of today and why

_____

_____

_____

_____

1 thing I learned today that I will help me grow

_____

_____

Free Flow Thoughts

Day   Date:

Good morning, today I start the day with gratitude and positive intentions.

How do I feel and how will I show myself some love?

_____

_____

1 thing I am grateful for this morning

_____

_____

I am grateful for this because

_____

_____

3 positive intentions for the day to **show myself love...**

1.

2.

3.

Reflect on the day, remember the positive and acknowledge the lessons.

1 thing I am proud of today and why

_____

_____

_____

_____

1 thing I learned today that I will help me grow

_____

_____

Free Flow Thoughts

Day   Date:

Good morning, today I start the day with gratitude and positive intentions.

How do I feel and how will I show myself some love?

_____

_____

1 thing I am grateful for this morning

_____

_____

I am grateful for this because

_____

_____

3 positive intentions for the day to **show myself love...**

1.

2.

3.

Reflect on the day, remember the positive and acknowledge the lessons.

1 thing I am proud of today and why

_____

_____

_____

_____

1 thing I learned today that I will help me grow

_____

_____

Free Flow Thoughts

Day   Date:

Good morning, today I start the day with gratitude and positive intentions.

How do I feel and how will I show myself some love?

_____

_____

1 thing I am grateful for this morning

_____

_____

I am grateful for this because

_____

_____

3 positive intentions for the day to **show myself love...**

1.

2.

3.

Reflect on the day, remember the positive and acknowledge the lessons.

1 thing I am proud of today and why

_____

_____

_____

_____

1 thing I learned today that I will help me grow

_____

_____

Free Flow Thoughts

Day   Date:

Good morning, today I start the day with gratitude and positive intentions.

How do I feel and how will I show myself some love?

_____

_____

1 thing I am grateful for this morning

_____

_____

I am grateful for this because

_____

_____

3 positive intentions for the day to **show myself love...**

1.

2.

3.

Reflect on the day, remember the positive and acknowledge the lessons.

1 thing I am proud of today and why

_____

_____

_____

_____

1 thing I learned today that I will help me grow

_____

_____

Free Flow Thoughts

Day   Date:

Good morning, today I start the day with gratitude and positive intentions.

How do I feel and how will I show myself some love?

_____

_____

1 thing I am grateful for this morning

_____

_____

I am grateful for this because

_____

_____

3 positive intentions for the day to **show myself love...**

1.

2.

3.

Reflect on the day, remember the positive and acknowledge the lessons.

1 thing I am proud of today and why

_____

_____

_____

_____

1 thing I learned today that I will help me grow

_____

_____

Free Flow Thoughts

www.ingramcontent.com/pod-product-compliance
Lightning Source LLC
LaVergne TN
LVHW051045080426
835508LV00019B/1720